NATURAL

simple land art through the seasons

F

FRANCES LINCOLN LIMITED

PUBLISHERS

NATURAL
text and photographs by Marc Pouyet

Originally published in France as *Artistes de Nature*
copyright © Éditions Plume de Carotte 2006

First published in the English language by
Frances Lincoln Limited
4 Torriano Mews, Torriano Avenue, London NW5 2RZ
www.franceslincoln.com

Designed by Sarah Slack
Translation by Phoebe Dunn

British Library Cataloguing in Publication Data
A catalogue record for this book is available from the British Library

ISBN 13: 978-0-7112-2994-5

Printed in China

9 8 7 6 5 4 3 2 1

introduction

Snow, ice, leaves, flowers, berries, sticks, branches, mud, pebbles, sand... this book suggests a number of simple abstract creations for you to make when you are out and about, using nothing but the natural materials to hand throughout the seasons. There is great pleasure to be had from creating something beautiful in the course of only a few minutes, and it is a particularly good way of opening a child's eyes to all the elements nature has to offer, to the variety of shapes, colours and textures.

All of this is directly inspired by an artistic movement. Imagine artists who in challenging the fine-art establishment and its values decided to ditch the traditional artists' studios and galleries and start creating out of doors. They worked surrounded by nature but sought to use it in a new way, no longer as a model but as a material in itself, in the full knowledge that their work would disappear with the passage of time.

Among these artists are Robert Smithson, who created a giant stone spiral jetty in America's Great Salt Lake, and Nils Udo, who makes giant, magical nests from birch trunks and willow branches – occasionally housing a small sleeping child.   Then there is Andy Goldsworthy, who creates delicate shapes with gradations of leaves, stones and earth or spheres of stone or wood.

In most cases, Land Art is modest and ephemeral – works created outside don't usually last long as they are subject to the elements; the wind, rain or snow that transforms and ultimately destroys them. But what remains is the pleasure of having created the work – and a photo of the creation is itself an integral part of the creative process, allowing the artist to keep proof of its momentary existence.

Land Art allows us all to express how we feel about nature. So this book's challenge is to inspire you to get out into nature and to create with it.

SPRING

SUMMER

AUTUMN

WINTER

SPRING

Fresh cherry branches between two pieces of granite.
Dandelions and moss on a rock.

Trefoil flowers neatly arranged on blocks of granite.

Daffodils drape themselves around the foot of a tree.

Branches of broom crown a block of granite.

Daffodils floating on the currents of a pond and snaking across mossy rocks.

A posy of marsh marigolds at the foot of a tree stump.
Daffodils around a log.

A two dimensional daisy-tree.
A leaf made of daisies and cow parsley...covered by broom...
and dotted with red campion.

FLOWERS

Which is the most fragile flower, or the strongest? That depends on
all sorts of factors like the time of day, temperature, how far in bloom
they are. Of course the poppy is so fragile you can only use its petals early
in the morning, Daisies and marsh marigolds are fairly robust.
It can be pleasant to work with dandelions too – particularly after they
have flowered, when each seed is topped with its short-lived, fluffy crest.

Primroses on a tree trunk, and mirroring the shadows thrown by a tree.
Dandelions along a grassy river bank.

SHADOW

As we well know, shadows move constantly. Lining up flowers or grasses along a shadow
has to be an exercise in speed and anticipation. Nevertheless, the almost inevitable
discrepancies you get in the lines themselves create unexpected and interesting patterns.

Spirals of daisy petals, primroses and dandelions.

A circle of dandelions held in place by ivy vines.
A dandelion cube (with a wire support) stands out in its meadow surroundings.

CREATION

I prefer to use just a single natural element in my creations –

a single type of flower or leaf. Attempts to use any more often

end up looking too decorative.

A line of dandelions across a stream is gradually joined by other flowers dropped in above the small waterfall.

Sticks emerging from the mud of a pond.

WATER
It's difficult to master water – a simple net or a small
wave can destroy a whole installation in a moment.
So I choose to work by peaceful rivers and streams,
calm ponds or small waterfalls.

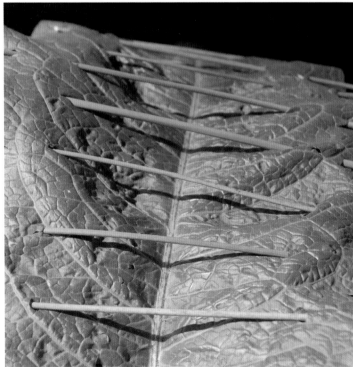

A cone of linden leaves and cut out shapes.
Rushes threaded through a sorrel leaf.
A cut-out lilac leaf against the night sky.

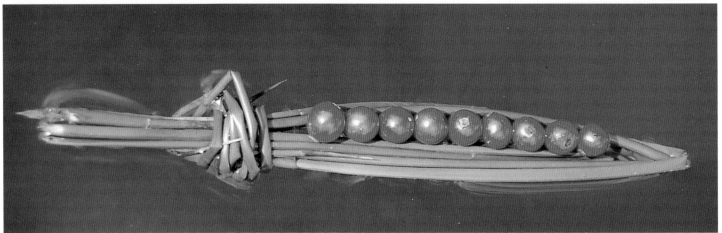

Floating holly berries and a raft of rushes.
Marsh marigolds with rushes, riding a raft of bark and floating on lichen.

PRECAUTIONS

Nature is welcoming but she is also full of tricks and dangers. Beware of
ice that burns, of ferns or couch grass that cut, or of mushrooms, berries
and flowers that seem so attractive yet are highly poisonous – amanitas,
honeysuckles, celandines, snowberries, mistletoe ...

Red campion flowers framed by a circle of stones.
Marsh marigolds form a pattern in the centre.

Dandelion clocks in various shapes await the breeze.

Fake branches and fungi made of clay.
A collection of dead branches at the foot of a large oak.

A ball of ivy stems watched by cattle.

Sunset through the ball of ivy.

Bracken on dead leaves.
Crosswort to make you cross eyed.

SUMMER

Brome and orchard grass: evening and morning.

LIGHT

The end of the afternoon or the early evening with its warm, gentle light is the best time for photos, even better than the full sun of midday or the early morning. Very grey or even rainy days can also provide a delicate atmosphere.

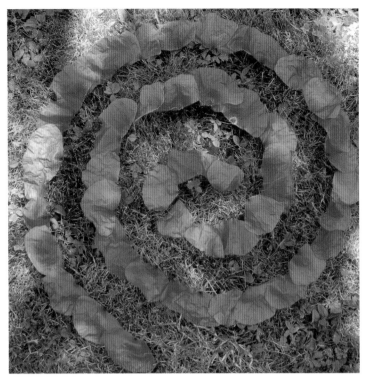

Poppy petals on grass, stone and fig leaf,
and threaded onto a poppy stem.

Dry grasses tied with fresh grass - order and chaos.

Cornflowers surround a reddening sorrel leaf, and
nestle between the granite stones in an old wall.

Cornflowers and a maple leaf.
Scabious, foxglove and cornflowers.
Cornflowers on an iris leaf against a backdrop of coronilla.

Cow parsley against green grass.
A mandala of mock orange, foxgloves, goosegrass, mallow and dandelion

Wild strawberries, strawberry leaves and elderflowers on a bed of moss.

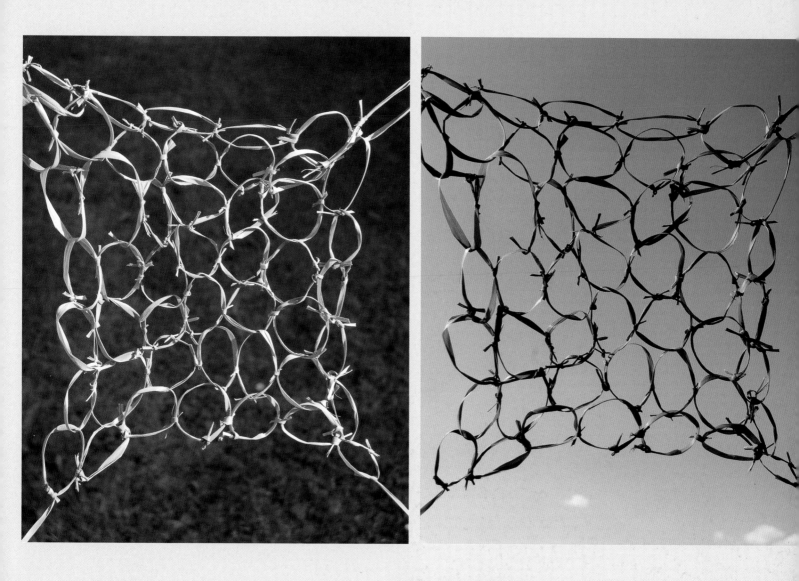

Webs of couch grass.

TOOLS

I needed very few tools for the creations in this book; just a knife and some secateurs. Or you can use the natural tools that come to hand wherever you are working: a shell-mould, a stone-hammer, a bark-bucket or a stick-pen.

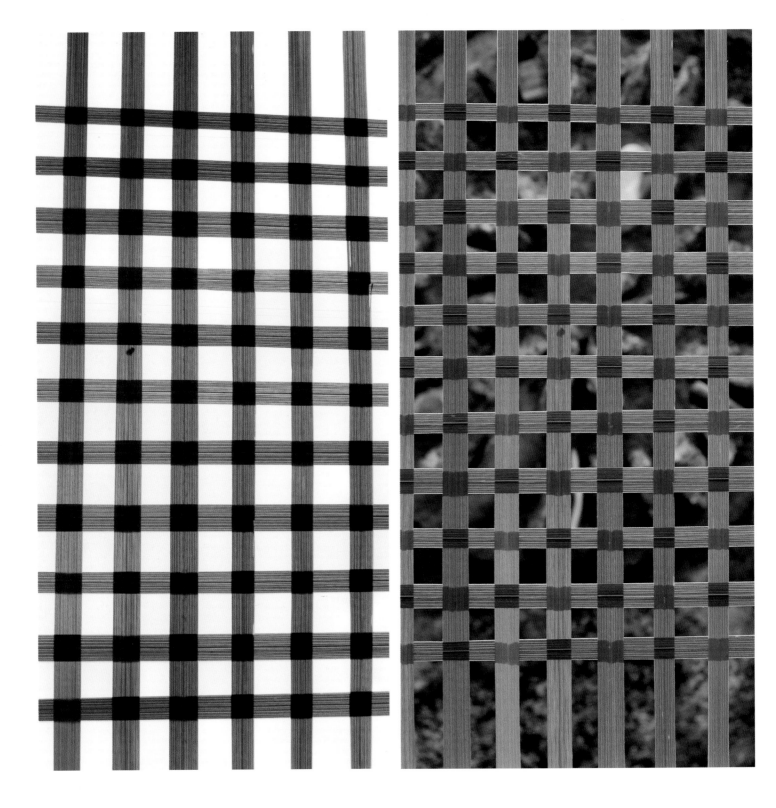

Woven couch grass.
Iris leaves and plum tree pins.

Feathers in the sunshine.
Overleaf: Arrangements of feathers from flamingos and birds of prey.

A curtain of branches hanging from a hazel arch forms an insubstantial barrier.
Cow parsley stems cut and threaded together.

Curtains of slender branches and foxgloves.

Zigzags in the wet sand.
Simple shapes and their shadows.

SAND

Sand is a constant source of inspiration: whether it's
wet or dry it presents a huge variety of colours and
textures. On your travels you can create a very rich
palette of white, ochre, red, brown. When creating
by the sea I work on the damp sand at low tide so as
not to leave any footprints.

A ball of rolled seaweed.
Varieties of seaweed displayed at the beach.

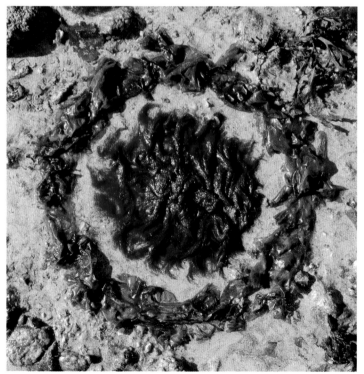

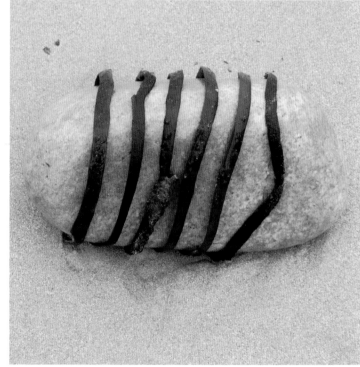

Pebbles on wet sand.
Wet black pebble footprints, and the footprints' prints.
Grey and gold sand

SEA

A tide table is an essential tool when you are
working on the Atlantic coast! Here more than
anywhere you have to be ready to bend to the
climatic conditions. Wind, rain, light all change
so quickly: you may have created a pebble
installation in the full sun – a study in greys -
but a few drops of rain later and you have
a pointillist picture. Some fine rain and the
light grey stones turn black, ochre and red.

Pale coloured pebbles are brought to life with some water.
An alignment of quartz veins in pebbles.
Patterns of granite, quartz and shale with terracotta
and coloured glass.

A procession of pebbles.
A stony smile.

Shell battlements and outlines.
Pebbles wedged into a larger stone.

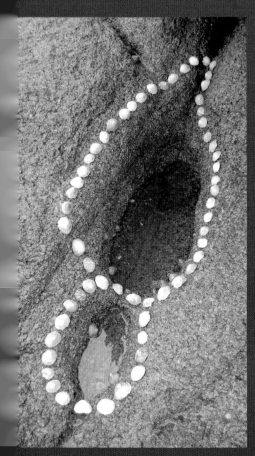

COLLECTING

Most often I create installations in response to the place, the conditions and the elements that I find. There is a real temptation to collect that little coloured pebble, that amazingly intricate leaf with the lovely markings or that funny shaped branch. But once these treasures are left back at the workshop you never have them to hand at the moment when you could have used them...

AUTUMN

Wood cranesbill leaves around an oak trunk.
A mossy bed for these small twigs.

Fluffy lichen & moss.

A circle of lichen surrounded in turn by moss, wood cranesbill leaves
and alder catkins.

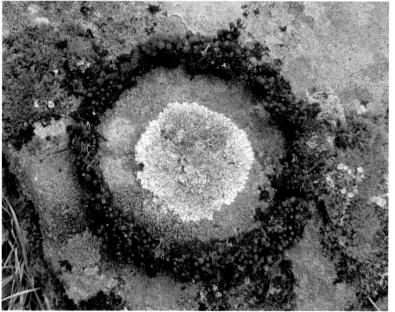

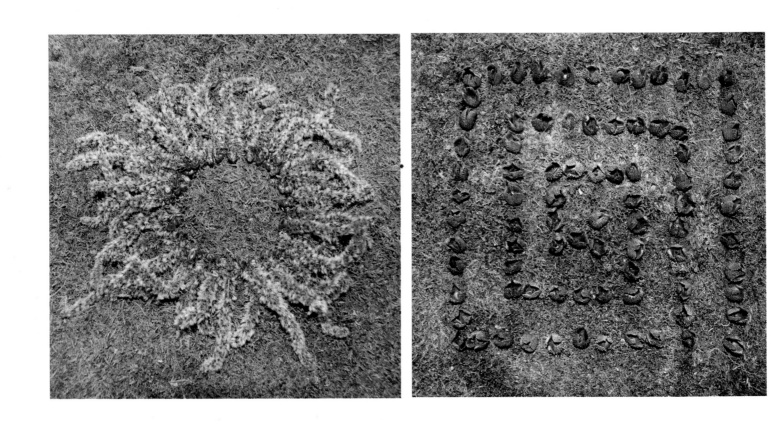

Poplar catkins and beech husks on moss.
A ball of beech husks.

Dried pine branches with fresh pine needles.

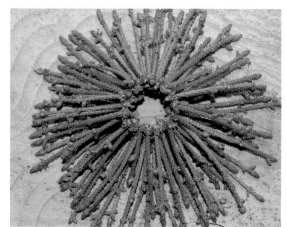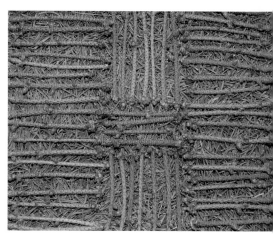

Pine needles trace the growth circles in this piece of wood.
Pine branches nestled in bark.

Dried chestnut leaves on a bed of lichen.
Dried chestnut leaves make a fish bone, and the whole fillet.

Maple leaves folded and held down with plum tree pins.
Poplar leaves and plum tree pins protecting the moss from the sun.

STICKING

You can use evergreen resin applied with pine needles to stick leaves
and flowers. You can also attach leaves or petals to stalks or stones
simply by moulding them.

Top to toe gingko leaves on a background of sweet cherry.
Patterns created by layering sweet cherry leaves and gingko.

Ivy leaves together – from green to dark and from smooth to veined.
Ivy – the autumn & winter collection.

Dry beech leaves.
Bramble leaves on moss.
Fresh beech leaves transparent in the sun.

A cube of maple leaves with their stems poking out,
held together by plum tree pins.

Hazel and alder catkins.
Wood cranesbill leaves turning red.

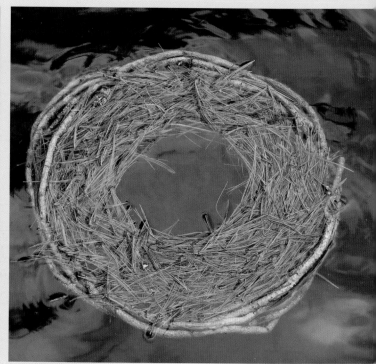

Pine needles and ivy stems gradually succumb to the current.

Maple and cow parsley shadows.
A pallet of Virginia creeper leaves.

COLOURS

Playing with shades of colours is always a temptation when you are trying

to create with natural elements. It reminds you of the infinite delicateness

and richness of nature.

WINTER

A frozen field framed by a block of snow.

Maple leaves on a freshly rolled snowball.

An oak branch cut into four sections, stripped and stuck back together with pine resin.

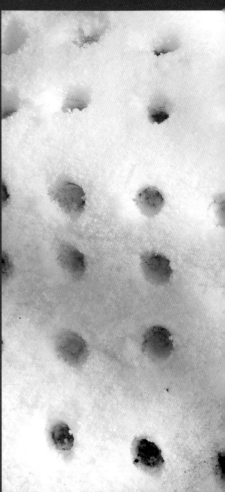

Patterns drawn with a twig in fresh snow on smooth and mossy stones,
and transforming a tree stump into a snow snail.

Catkins on snow.

Naturally coloured snowballs placed on bare branches.
To colour snow red you can crush Guelder rose berries in a
little water and pour over a firm snowball. The green was
achieved with wild garlic and the yellow with concentrated
lemon juice (cheating slightly).

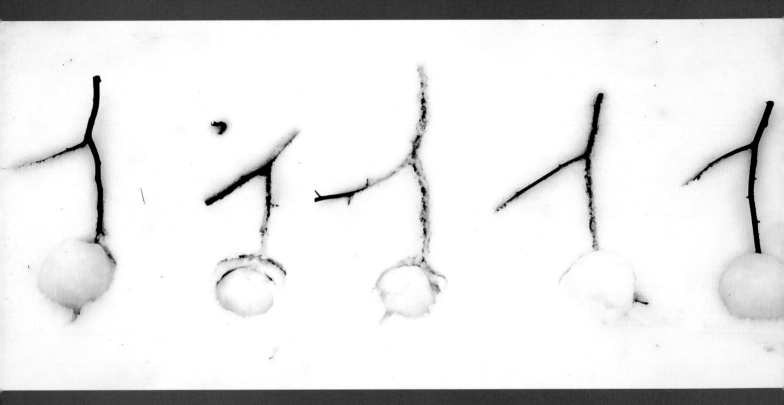

Softening snowballs sink into their snowy carpet.
Fresh snow packed into the hollow of a tree trunk.

SNOW

Early in the morning, when I discover it's snowed overnight I can't wait
to set to work but I almost always have to wait till the temperature has
risen towards the end of the morning. Any earlier and the snow can be
so powdery that it's sometimes impossible to even make a snowball.

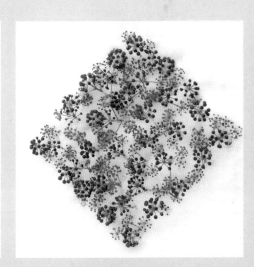

Pieces of wood, catchfly heads, twigs and ivy berries carefully arranged on snow.

Melting snow on a background of yellow grass.
A track left where the snow has been lifted by a giant snowball.

Held in place by two hazel pegs, an arrangement of delicate
twigs frames the view of a frosty field.

Sections of willow create an explosion on the melting snow.

Laurel leaves with plum tree pins.

Melting ice on beech leaves.

Shards on a sheet of ice.

ICE

Like the many kinds of snow, wind or light,
nature gives us an infinite variety of ice – thin,
translucent, milky, tough, fragile... Any rigidly
pre-planned project is doomed to failure. You have
to adapt to the conditions of the moment, using
the natural elements to hand according to their
momentary characteristics.

Hazel catkins and wood cranesbill leaves on frosty ice.
A stem frozen into the ice with wood cranesbill flowers
placed on top..

Slabs of ice carefully arranged along a bare branch.

A block of ice frozen to a tree trunk by quickly freezing water.

Willow branches in a ball of fluffy lichen.

Ferns and poplar leaves on a piece of granite, itself pattered with lichen.

Circles of moss cut out and stuck to a tree trunk.
A rotten birch branch with sections of bark cut away.

An ivy leaf becomes a butterfly placed next to two small twigs.
An ivy stem shifted on its host trunk, and a peeled stick against a dark trunk.

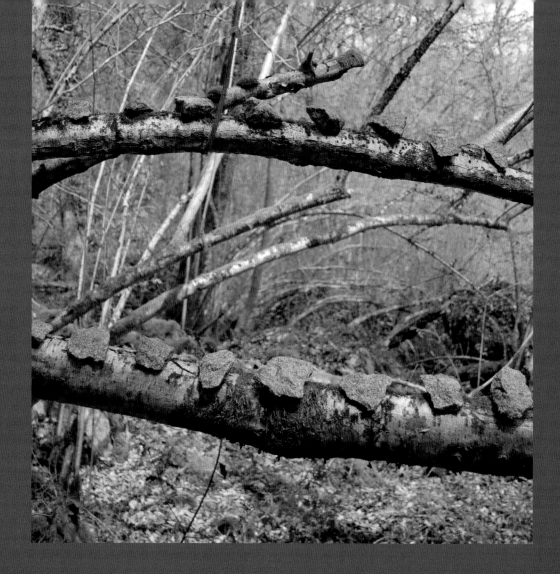

Granite stones balancing on birch branches.
Rounded granite stones nestle between two trunks.

STONES
These granite stones – shards from an ancient quarry long-reclaimed
by nature - were abandoned by the 'Masons of the Creuse' who left
their homes on the north-western border of the Massif Central to help
build Paris and other French cities.

acknowledgements

In my work with nature before the installations and photos in this book I had tended to be primarily an observer. I was happy to observe the variety of scenes mother nature shows us - some small scale and others large, some of them unremarkable and others extraordinary, but nearly all of them short-lived and fleeting.

The aim of this project, suggested by my original French publishers Frédéric Lisak and the Plume de Carotte team, was that I should intervene directly in nature and create installations using nothing but natural materials. I quickly understood what a shift that would require...

There were so many possible materials and I had so many ideas, so I set about working in accordance with the seasons, the weather and whatever natural elements I found.

I will always be grateful to my native region of Creuse with its natural treasures, the richness and variety of its plants and flowers, its beauty, the freedom to roam through its countryside, and of course the welcome and the understanding of its people. Thanks to the Limousin mountains and the Millevaches plateau. Thank you to my Creuse.

My beach work was done in Brittany on the Côte de granit rose (the pink granite coast), which like the Creuse region has plenty of granite. What a magical place, what light... Other work took place in the southwest between Haute Garonne and Gers – another area of endless possibilities. Nature is so full of discoveries, explorations and creations – let us respect it and work to preserve it.

I must also thank all my helpers – friends and co-workers – who helped me both with the heavy work and with the detail.

I hope that these pictures will make you want to work with and have fun with nature and create your own land art.